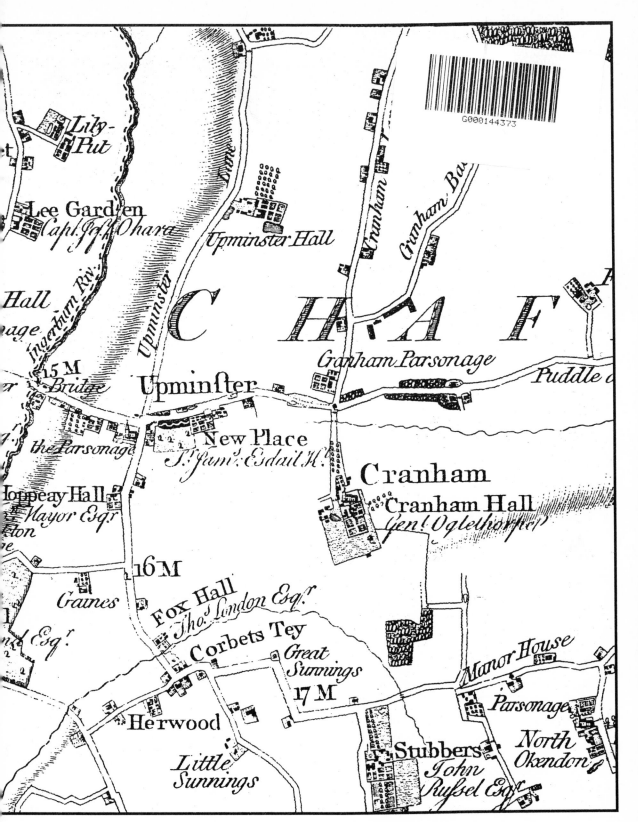

Hornchurch and Upminster on the Chapman and André map, 1777.

BYGONE
HORNCHURCH
and UPMINSTER

BYGONE
HORNCHURCH
and UPMINSTER

Brian Evans

Phillimore

1990

Published by
PHILLIMORE & CO. LTD.
Shopwyke Hall, Chichester, Sussex

ISBN 0 85033 754 2

Printed and bound in Great Britain by
BIDDLES LTD.
Guildford, Surrey

To all my friends in Hornchurch and Upminster

List of Illustrations

Acknowledgements

The author would like to thank the following for all the help they have given with either the text or the illustrations: George Berry, Mrs. F. Caldwell, Mr. H. H. Cook, Havering Libraries, Mrs. Barbara Mannox, Roy Squire, Mrs. Tyler and Mrs. J. Wheal.

Introduction

Hornchurch: Village of the Bull's Head

The site Hornchurch now occupies can be traced back to the time when it lay at the southern edge of the ice sheet covering Britain during the Ice Age. Later a great river flowed from west to east through this landscape, long before the Thames was formed. Evidence for this was revealed in the geological strata uncovered by workmen when the Romford to Upminster railway line was being constructed in 1893. Much later the Thames flowed over this area, gradually cutting its way down through a series of terraces before descending into its present level.

Evidence of early human occupation in Hornchurch has been found near St Andrew's church. Tools and implements discovered belong to the Mousterian culture, a period associated with primitive Neanderthal man. This culture began to disappear at the beginning of the last Ice Age, the people first withdrawing into cave shelters to avoid the increasing cold and later migrating south as conditions worsened. Man returned to the area in Neolithic times, and remains have been discovered at Rainham and elsewhere in the vicinity. The dense deciduous forest at that time, full of animals for hunting, provided shelter, food and clothing.

The Romans constructed the great highway to Colchester, clearing the woodland on what became Hornchurch's northern boundary. Evidence of Roman occupation has been discovered at Mardyke Farm, near the River Beam. Even earlier than this there had been local religious sites. One of these was on the small hilltop where St Andrew's church now stands. An early British trackway connected Ilford and Barking, where there were also early religious centres, with Hornchurch, Upminster and probably Horndon. All these sites were probably centres of pre-Christian worship; the Druids may well have celebrated their rites here, including the sacrifice of bulls. This may account for the incorporation of the word 'horn' into local place names in the early medieval period. Further reinforcement of this symbol as a local icon occurred when monks from the St Nicholas and St Bernard monastery at Montjoux in Savoy were invited by King Henry II to set up a small Priory in Hornchurch in 1158/9; the mother house was designated *Cornutem Monasterium*, or the 'Horned Monastery'. It may even have been built on the spot where there had earlier been a temple to Diana, using the symbolism of the bull's head.

In the Middle Ages the village was becoming an important centre of the leather trade, and this, too, would have been a factor in the use of the bull's head and horns as a local badge and symbol. In a royal charter of Henry II the church at Hornchurch was still called 'Ecclesia de Havering' (as it was the main church of the royal manor) but by 1253, when Henry III granted a charter, the designation 'Cornutem Monasterium' was given to the daughter house of the Priory for the first time.

Medieval Hornchurch seems to have been a busy and prosperous place, with a surprising number of named streets considering the size of the village. The High Street was at that time called Pell Street or Pelt Street, and its distinctive double bow shape has altered little over the centuries. This name reflects the fact that as early as the 12th century a considerable amount of currying and leather dressing was being done in the village. There were tan yards in the fields behind the old *King's Head Inn* as well as others along the present High Street. Lake Street (Lakestrate in 1285) may correspond to Station Lane, for there was apparently a large pool in this area in earlier times. Hythelane, mentioned in 1497, refers to a landing place on the River Ingrebourne – perhaps some of Hornchurch's leather goods were taken out of the town in this way, though much was sold at Romford Market on the great Essex road. Lychelane, mentioned in 1411 and 1503, derives from the Old English for a corpse and refers to a road near the graveyard, perhaps even the hill up to the church itself, afterwards known as Church Hill and more recently part of the High Street. Other roads mentioned in early documents are Westlane (1237), Smithesstrate (1341) and Hureleslane (1376). The last name is intriguing as there have been Hurrells living in the locality in recent times.

As the centuries progressed, Hornchurch gained popularity with prominent people and surviving monuments in the church testify to the number of crown and law officials who found the area a congenial and convenient place to rest from their arduous duties in London. Some, like Thomas Witherings, however, seemed to find little rest as they were always devising new schemes and business ventures. Witherings was involved in the establishment of the first State postal service in England and Scotland. He was in effect the earliest Postmaster General but business and personal worries during the troubled Civil War days caused him to have a stroke in 1649 and he died on his way to church at St Andrew's on 28 September 1651. He lies buried in the chancel of the church, where he was an elder. The memorial on the wall describes him as: 'second to none for unfathomed poilesicy, unparralled sagacious and divining Genius; witness his great correspondence in all parts of ye Christian World.'

Upminster: Village in the Meadows

Upminster church is thought to have been founded some time after A.D. 653, when Cedd, brother of St Chad, was sent to preach and baptise in Essex and made his headquarters at nearby Tilbury and at Ithancester (now Bradwell) where he built St Peter's-on-the-Wall, the first church in Essex, still standing today. Upminster's first church would have been a simple shrine of wood or wattle and daub, built in a clearing in the great forest which then covered Essex. Its parish would have covered an extensive area, as it became mother church to many others over a period of time. During the reign of King John (1199-1216), when the Minster-on-the-Hill had become a more permanent structure and the Engayne family had come into the possession of the manor of Gaines, the church was rebuilt in stone – the two lower stages of the present tower date from that time.

In the Middle Ages the church at Upminster was only a few miles from the royal palace at Havering and so had an enhanced appeal to fugitives seeking sanctuary and protection. Sanctuary was an ancient privilege dating from A.D. 597. King Ethelbert confirmed the sanctity of churches, ruling that any violation of 'Church-Frith', as it was termed, should be punished by a fine double that of an ordinary breach of the King's Peace. Later those who breached this rule faced excommunication.

A record of a local sanctuary case dating from the 1260s is in the Assize Roll at the Public Record Office and reads as follows:

> Hugh the merchant, taxed and prosecuted for theft made in the cowshed of William de Stokes by a certain Andrew Wynter, fled to the Church of Upmenstre, & acknowledged the theft and abjured the realm before the coroner.

Those sworn to abjure the realm (i.e. to be banished from the country) as a punishment had to go straight to the port of departure determined by the coroner, swearing 'I schal not goe out of ye hygh weye'. Such men were not the only travellers well advised to keep to the main highway in medieval Essex. Farm workers and even those living in Upminster itself needed to be on the alert when on the road. The woodland and forest still supported hungry wolves and other wild animals. As late as the reign of Henry VII (1485-1509) the Crown was concerned to exterminate the wolves which were still making depredations among the people and their livestock. The owners of estates had to pay a tax for this, assessed in terms of corpses. Sunnings in Upminster, for instance, was assessed for three wolves while Stubbers was only rated for two.

Some consolation for the harshness of daily life in the Middle Ages was brought by visits to the parish church on Sundays and holy days. The painted walls, stained glass windows, elaborate vestments and fine plate, together with the familiar rituals and the hope of a better life in the hereafter, brought colour and cheer into people's lives. There were also the Church Ales, festivals with entertainments provided by the church. The people of Upminster were also fortunate to live close to the land in a beautiful swathe of countryside, cut off from some of the worst ills of urban life. Some measure of the rural past survived into the 19th century. Wilson, historian of the village, writes in his *Sketches of Upminster*:

> Sounds are floating over the distant trees and we discern the slender spire and massy tower of Hornchurch, whence the music that regaled our ears as we approached this spot [Hacton]. On the other side of the bridge, in the meadow, we find the grass twinkling in the sun, daisies opening their eyes, and buttercups gleaming in profusion.

Green Mansions

There was a surprising continuity in life on the farms and in the countryside around Hornchurch and Upminster throughout the centuries and up to the period immediately after the Second World War. There was continuity in families, land ownership, buildings and in methods of working the land. Changes occurred, but only slowly.

When Henry II gave around 1,500 acres of land in 1158/9 to the Hospital of St Nicholas and St Bernard at Montjoux in Savoy to found Hornchurch Priory he was establishing a pattern of land ownership in large blocks which endured for centuries. Some of these holdings are marked on the 1618 map of the Liberty; the central Hornchurch section reproduced as plate 4 reveals a portion of this land. The monks of Montjoux were succeeded in 1385 by New College, Oxford as owners of this land and hundreds of documents in the College archives record changes in holdings and the names of tenants. Most of the land over which Hornchurch Airfield later spread belonged to Suttons Manor and was part of the original grant to the Priory. No fewer than 547 documents relating to local land are listed in a Kalendar of New College; many names of places and people are still recognisable today – Aps (Abbs Cross), Dovers (Corner), Haketoneland (Hactons) and Colbeshatch (perhaps Corbets Tey).

The sites of farms were established in Saxon and Norman times and often the same buildings would stand for centuries. Many farm buildings were altered and added to over the years and other structures were renewed completely above ground but the building rested on the foundations of several earlier houses. Bretons is a surviving example of this. The Chapman and André map of 1777 shows graphically the landscape of 18th-century Hornchurch and Upminster. The farms and great houses are spread out in a 'sea' of countryside, served by a sparse network of roads. The farms were often approached by their own 'chase' or farm lane leading for some considerable distance from the public road. A large number of these isolated buildings survived into the present century, only to be swept away by a torrent of so-called progress. These include the Chaplaincy (whose Victorian exterior was found to contain an ancient timber wall with wattle and daub infill), Hornchurch Hall (damaged during the war), Hoppy Hall, Londons, Stubbers, Fox Hall, New Place, Gerpins, Hunts, Nelmes, Ayletts, Bright's Farm, Bush Elms, Redden Court, Wych Elm and Suttons Gate. This long list of lost heritage makes the buildings which have survived, many of them originally farmhouses, even more precious. Among the survivors, Bretons has already been mentioned, probably owing its survival to its employment as the headquarters of a sewage farm. Others are Upminster Hall, Great Sunnings, Berwick Manor, Bramble Farm, Cranham Hall, High House, Capel Nelmes, Tylers Hall, Fairkytes, Langtons, Sullens, Albyns, Tadlows, Old Cottage, Franks, Pages, Great Tomkyns and Lilliputs. A few other outstanding buildings connected with the area's agricultural past have survived. These include two 16th-century brick barns at Bretons, the smock mill at Upminster with its original machinery and the superb tithe barn in Hall Lane. This is believed to date from the late 14th century, has exceptionally interesting features and is now scheduled as an Ancient Monument.

In July 1812 a return was made to Parliament which showed that 197 of a total of 319 families in Hornchurch (over 60 per cent) were employed in agriculture; the proportion for Upminster was even higher. Since 1784 there had been a manufactory of agricultural implements in Billet Lane, Hornchurch, on a site which later reverted to green fields and now contains the modern Queen's Theatre. The manufactory had been founded by two brothers, Thomas and Robert Wedlake. On Thomas's death his widow and son-in-law carried on the original business while Robert founded a rival company in Hornchurch High Street, known as the Union Foundry. Mary Wedlake continued to sell patent implements, many of which had been invented by Robert. She advertised her products extensively in newspapers and also produced very attractive pocket catalogues in the mid-19th century.

One farm which continued in its old buildings until after the last war was Damyns Hall, south of the area covered in this book. It is officially in Rainham parish but looked to Upminster for many facilities. This old building is recorded in a document of 1545 as Damyans, the name deriving from the family of William Damyon, but it probably originated much earlier under another name, it being the custom for farms to take the name of their owner or occupier. Joan Paveley, now Mrs. Wheal, remembers the farm in the 1940s. Her grandfather George Paveley, like his father before him, had begun as a horseman to farmer Vellacott who owned several farms in the area. George eventually became the tenant at Damyns, as did his son Edward after him. In Edward's day the farm was largely run by women, including his daughter Joan, her two aunts and a cousin. Edward's attitude was that 'if he could do it, so could they'. At 16, Joan was not heavy enough to balance the iron one-furrow plough so her father hung two 56 lb weights on the handle. Damyns was mainly devoted to market gardening at that time, but there were also about 200 pigs, three horses, chickens and ducks. Although most of the farm was on clay, the piggeries and stables were on a chalk outcrop and so hearth-whitening stone was freely available. The farmhouse had many unusual features, including a back kitchen paved with cobbles. Behind the main kitchen was a well, 10 ft. deep, completely reliable and fed by a local spring. Other wells in the yard could be opened up and brought into use in dry years. It was very difficult to make Damyns pay in the 1950s and Edward Paveley eventually gave up the farm, retiring to Cranham. Two weeks later, in 1956, the farm buildings burned down. The farm has now been incorporated into the larger holding of neighbouring farmer Mr. Watt. Twelve of Damyns old fields, the largest of which was 17 acres, have now become three large fields, as dictated by modern farming practices. Damyns is not the only example of the late survival of an ancient farm, but it provided a tangible link with the distant past, continuing into the 20th century a way of life which had been typical in the Essex countryside for hundreds of years.

Evidence of the popularity and rapid growth of both Hornchurch and Upminster is provided by the population statistics. At the end of the 18th century Upminster was a rural village of only 200 inhabitants, but by 1961 it was home to almost 15,000 people. Hornchurch, its larger neighbour, had only 1,331 inhabitants in 1801. Its population rose to 9,361 by 1911 and the surge in house building in the inter-war period brought numbers to 28,417 in 1931. Boundary extensions brought Hornchurch's population to the huge figure of 131,014 by 1961.

Hornchurch:
Village of the Bull's Head

1. Hornchurch's venerable church as it appeared in 1823 and for centuries before, surrounded by fields and woodland. Because it stood on a hill, ships on the Thames could use the spire as a point of reference and this fact saved it from demolition around 1800. For the same reason Trinity House contributed towards its repair.

2. Hornchurch Priory seal with its bull's head design is attached to a document in New College, Oxford dated 1385. The Priory stood on the same ridge as the church, but probably lay to the north.

3. Charter of Henry II (1158) granting 'to the poor of Montjoux in the church of St Nicholas and St Bernard land at Havering worth £25 a year'. When the monks were ejected, their lands were acquired by William of Wykeham who founded New College, Oxford and used the income from the lands and property of the priory to endow it. Consequently, a wealth of documents on medieval Hornchurch are preserved in New College archives.

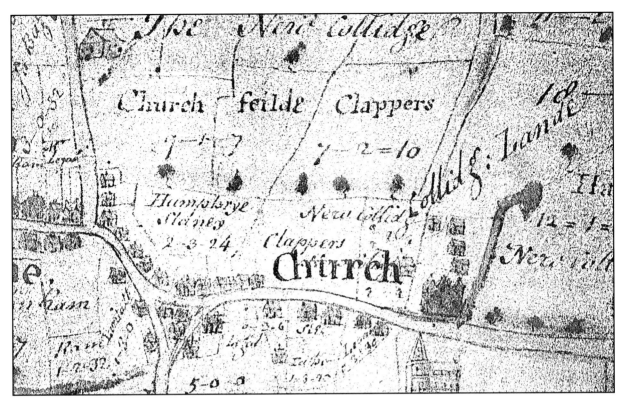

4. A section of the 1618 Map of the Liberty of Havering. The original is on animal skin. It includes representations of buildings and land holders, including the Rame family who have a memorial in the church.

5. An engraving of the 19th-century church showing the bull's horns at the east end and a wooden grave marker. Several such markers were to be seen in Upminster and Hornchurch churchyards.

6. A view of the natural arena behind the church known as the Dell. This probably originated as a quarry and later became a recreation ground for the village. Water, trees and turf made it a very attractive area around the turn of the century.

7. Bamford's view of the interior of St Andrew's, showing a wealth of detail, including the altar tomb of William Ayloffe under the arch at the left. Other links with Ayloffe's era are the brick barns he built as owner of 'Bretense' manor, as it was described on the tomb.

8. (*left*) Bamford drew the carving in the turret in 1896. It is thought to represent William of Wykeham, Bishop of Winchester. Chancellor and T. L. Wilson were of the opinion that Wykeham was responsible for the perpendicular portions of the church, especially the tower. (*right*) Stained glass representation of a royal figure, believed to be Edward the Confessor, possibly dating from 1404-8 when 167ft. of stained glass was commissioned for the three chancel windows. This Bamford drawing was made in 1890.

The Figure is about 19 in. high.

Alf Bennett Bamford
Sept. 1896

Old Corner, High Street, Hornchurch.

9. The *Britannia Inn* in the High Street exhibited all the signs of once having been an ecclesiastical building of some importance. It was probably the site of a hospice where monks provided for weary travellers and pilgrims and dispensed other charitable alms to the poor. The building extended into North Street where, at its eastern end, there was a large chimney stack and part of a flank wall constructed entirely of Kentish Ragstone.

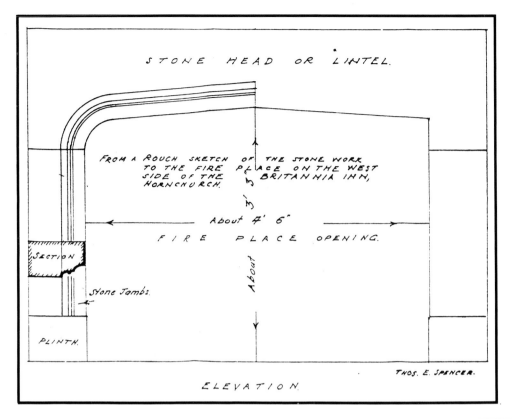

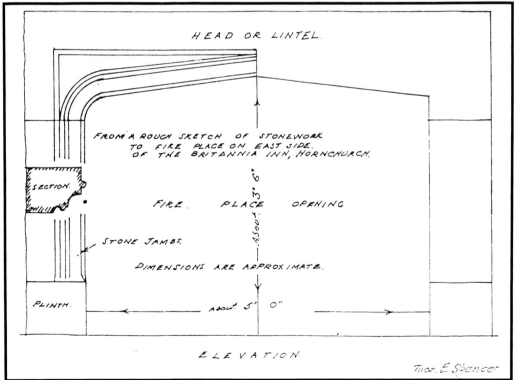

10. Although no longer an inn, the *Britannia* building lingered on into the late 1930s. During demolition shortly before the outbreak of the Second World War, two stone fireplaces were discovered behind Victorian grates, one at either end of the hall-type building. T. E. Spencer made a drawing of these and suggested that pilgrims on their way to Canterbury may have been accommodated and refreshed here.

11. Humphrey Pye, commemorated by this wall monument in the church, is an example of the many notable persons who came to live in the district. He is described as 'a Citizen and Writer of the Courte Letter of London, and Attorney of the Common Pleas at Westminster'. He died a bachelor, aged 57, in 1625.

12. Brasses of Thomas Drywood and his wife of 28 years. Thomas was also 57 when he died in 1591. There are two mutilated brasses in the church to Humphrey and William Drywood of the same family, who died in 1595 and 1602 respectively. Effigies of the two wives of William are set in a modern slab.

13. Maylands or Maylerds Green, Hornchurch, where the Drywoods once lived, pictured in the late 19th century. Originally named after the family of Geoffrey Le Meilur who appears in documents dated 1240, it is shown on Norden's map of 1594. In a 1674 deed the Drywood family is associated with it and it is described as 'Drywoods in the Lane alias Maylands alias Maylands Green'.

14. Wykeham Cottages, Church Hill, 1919. 'Two cottages called Painters Almshouses derived from the gift of Anthony Ram in 1699 being in a dilapidated state were let in 1824, for 31 years at the annual rent of £10 to two lessees, each of whom covenanted to expend £200 in rebuilding the houses' (White). The two cottages are now converted into one dwelling. Anthony was the son of Francis mentioned in the next caption. The family name is variously spelt Ram or Rame.

MONUMENT TO
FRANCIS RAME
HORNCHURCH CHURCH.

15. Monument to Francis Rame, 1617, Steward to Sir Anthony Cooke of Gidea Hall, with its two principal figures and ten children kneeling underneath. The splendour of this monument and others in the church demonstrates what prosperous times Hornchurch enjoyed between the 16th and 18th centuries.

16. Thomas Witherings of Great Nelmes is commemorated in a monument in the church of 1651. For a few years Witherings was Postmaster General and ran the posts 'night and day', greatly speeding up deliveries. Thomas had gained this appointment as a result of knowledge acquired while serving as 'Harbinger' to the Queen which required him to proceed ahead of the Court, organising secure lodgings and temporary postal arrangements.

17.   A side view of Hornchurch Hall which lay back from the road, where the Robert Beard Youth Club is now sited.

18.   Group photograph of the Gill family of Hornchurch Hall in the early 1900s. Back row, left to right: Nancy Gill (m. Leonard Eve of Cranham Hall), Lilian Poupart of Dovers (m. John Gill), Walter Vellacott, Elizabeth Vellacott (née Gill), Harry Gill (m. Ida Spear), Leonard Gill. Front row, left to right: John Gill (secretary of Essex Farmers Union, organised Essex Show), Mabel Stone (née Gill, of Cranham Hall), Walter Soaper Gill (of Hornchurch Hall, Elm Farm and later West Thurrock), his wife Elizabeth Gill (née Harris), Harry Stone (farmed Wennington), Margaret Vellacott. Children: unnamed cousin and Margaret Vellacott.

19. Ancient buildings opposite Billet Lane with the *Cricketers Inn* in the background. Notice the continuous fence on the right enclosing the Grey Towers land. The local resident sitting outside is making the most of the light and air and perhaps the chance to catch up on local gossip. Because the old houses were so dark and cramped, sitting out was a common practice.

20. Burnthouse Corner in the 1920s. Burnthouse Wood and Cottage are depicted on various 19th-century maps. This photograph shows a remarkably rural aspect apart from the lamp post and the advertisement for Flacks (gardeners).

21. These old buildings, dating from the 16th century, stood on the bend of the High Street. Perfect's *History* records a rather romantic story relating to the old barn at the back of the archway, involving a character named Jimmy Wood who robbed the Royal Mail on the High Road to Essex. He was shot but escaped and his mother hid him in the barn, nursing him back to health.

22. This cottage in North Street, Hornchurch, was built in the 17th century. In 1917 it was occupied by nurses from the New Zealand Convalescent Hospital but it was demolished in 1960 after a fire.

23.   In the open fields to the south of the parish, once a rather windswept and lonely area, stands the ancient Bretons Manor site. Successive houses are known to have stood here. Today an interesting Palladian-style farmhouse can still be seen. Even older is this Tudor barn, built by William Ayloffe at the back of the house, here portrayed by Bamford in 1889.

24.   Watercolour study of the *Harrow Inn*, Hornchurch, which was very well placed for the refreshment of travellers and workers in the fields nearby.

Upminster:
Village in the Meadows

25.   A wonderful engraving of Upminster church in 1793. St Lawrence's rises out of a peaceful green landscape where time appears to stand still. The village was noted for the longevity of its inhabitants. Wilson quoted a list of 20 nonagenarians (average age 92¾ years) who had been buried here in the 19th century.

26. Two ex-inhabitants of Upminster. (*left*) Brass of an unknown lady, *c.*1555. (*below*) Effigies in stained glass of Adrian D'Ewes and his wife Alice. Adrian came into England from the Duchy of Gelderland in the time of Henry VIII.

27. William Derham, D.D., F.R.S., Rector of Upminster, a unique combination of divine and scientist whose experiments and observations advanced the cause of British science and invention. He wrote papers on many subjects including the barometer, the great storm of 1703, astronomy, habits of the death watch beetle and wasps, and the migration of birds.

TABLE I.

A Table, shewing how many Pounds, and Centesimals of a Pound *Troy* of Rain, fell at *Towneley* in *Lancashire*, and at *Upminster* in *Essex*, in each Month of the Years 1699, &c. with the Quantity and Depth every Year.

	1699.		1700.		1701.		1702.	
	Townl.	*Upmr.*	*Townl.*	*Upmr.*	*Townl.*	*Upmr.*	*Townl.*	*Upmr.*
January	17 9	8 91	20 84	3 91	22 41	14 96	21 10	9 81
Febru.	32 70	60 5	19 12	7 64	16 78	8 78	21 27	7 30
March	17 92	5 63	7 58	1 55	7 10	3 91	2 48	2 37
April	10 47	3 44	18 65	7 60	6 11	1 43	5 34	10 90
May	4 00	2 67	17 92	6 91	19 67	9 11	8 81	6 49
June	10 37	46	13 15	7 60	11 34	5 79	23 00	13 46
July	16 51	6 36	15 26	4 24	17 58	9 49	25 31	4 39
August	19 77	8 57	12 05	8 14	23 66	6 57	20 12	6 88
Septem.	16 53	8 06	23 52	14 85	21 30	5 63	23 01	8 05
October	18 90	13 49	26 44	17 15	24 59	10 21	28 57	7 92
Novem.	14 65	1 91	13 69	5 24	25 60	8 22	37 11	14 05
Decem.	16 78	5 77	26 88	10 30	10 19	9 35	41 63	10 27
Total	196 51	75 55	215 30	95 13	206 33	93 45	257 75	101 89
Depth	39 302	15 110	43 060	19 026	41 266	18 696	51 55	20 378

28.   A scene in leafy Hall Lane in about 1912. A cow is being led from one field to another while a steam roller is awaiting employment, though surely not in Hall Lane itself.

29. 'A venerable mansion standing a measured mile north of the church – the hereditary abode of the Branfil family for nearly two centuries' (Wilson). Upminster Hall: (*above*) the exterior in about 1920; (*below*) the interior in 1880.

30. A beautifully framed view of the corner of Bird Lane and Hall Lane. The Edwardian family group is standing not far from what was Upminster's largest single source of employment – the Pot Kilns.

31. A page from Wilson's *History* showing the Brick Kiln in Bird Lane, built by Mr. Patrick in 1774, and giving its dimensions.

32.   Upminster Common at the turn of the century. The photograph appears to show recreational activities on a Sunday.

33. Upminster crossroads in 1880. The smithy at the side of Cranham Road (St Mary's Lane) looks surprisingly serene and peaceful, as does the entire scene. On the left is Cosy Corner at the entrance to Station Road, on the right the *Bell Inn*. All these buildings are standing on what was once open village green.

34. About 30 years later, little has changed as the photographer records the view up Station Road, with the prominent tower of the National School.

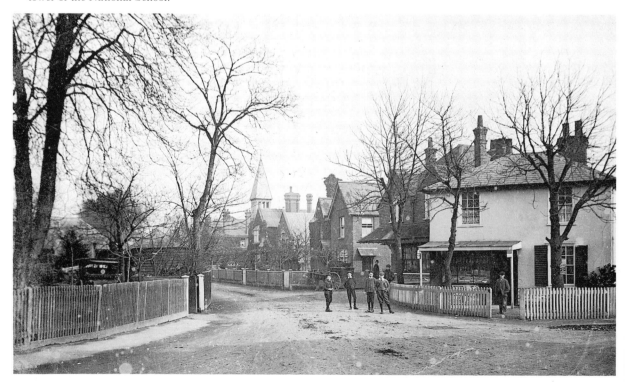

35. The *Bell Hotel* in Corbets Tey Road in the early years of this century. This rebuilt inn stands on part of the former village green. The original building stood 40 yards to the south-east. In front lay part of the green with a sweeping entrance lane to the inn. Sir James Esdaile was responsible for the re-alignment.

36. The first building down the lane itself was High House which was thought in 1880 to be three centuries old. Doctor Derham lived here because the old Rectory was in a poor condition. Later Major Howard, who died at Waterloo, was visited here by Lord Byron.

37. A westward view of the crossroads in 1907, with the Essex Hunt about to set off on a wet day.

38. Many of the houses in old Upminster were known by the name of the occupier. This house, 'Tadlows', was known as 'Rolfs' in 1704 when it stood in grounds of 40 acres. By 1720 it was 'Peacocks'. Mr. Tadlow was a superintendent of improvements for Sir James Esdaile, and worked on the grounds of Gaines Park.

39. Corbets Tey Road in slumber, its houses discreetly hidden behind the hedges and trees on the right, with open fields on the left.

40. The *George Inn* was known earlier as the *Royal George* after the King. In *Pigot's Directory* of 1835 it is the *George and Dragon*. An early licensee was Grace Sutton in 1769. George Stevens was landlord from 1788 until 1831 and was also gamekeeper at Gaines. His widow Ann continued the work until 1842 when she was 95; she contributed to Upminster's longevity record by living to be one hundred.

41. The old forge at Corbets Tey stood next to the *George* and is here photographed from the shadow of the *Huntsman and Hounds*.

42. This vehicle in Corbets Tey between the wars was probably a mobile shop. Note the sign advertising 'Teas' outside a garden on the left.

43. A large white house and this terrace in Corbets Tey were probably named after Joseph Keeling or some member of his family. He was Surveyor of Highways for the South Ward of Upminster in 1766.

44. Upminster Mill at the beginning of the First World War. The business was on the brink of decline because of government controls and the growth of large-scale milling.

45. Mr. Abraham, the last miller of Upminster, inside the mill in 1935. The Abrahams had been millers for generations but by this time the mill was up for sale and faced possible demolition.

46. A horseman on the bridge that divided Upminster and Hornchurch. This photograph was taken by Frank Luff who never went anywhere without his camera.

47. Bamford drew the 'remains of Hactons now used as a barn' in July 1890. Built by William Braund in the early 18th century, the house is described by Wilson as a 'spacious, well-proportioned red brick building with stone quoins and dressings'.

48. Park Corner Farm in about 1905. The farm acquired its name because of its proximity to Gaines Park. At this time it had been recorded as a farm for over two centuries and probably dated from an even earlier period. The attractive house with its iron railings, Regency gateposts, blinds and curtains has a cared-for appearance. The people outside may be members of the Knight family.

49. Upminster Bridge and the *Bridge House* tavern, 1904. An adjoining farm known as 'Briggehous' is recorded as early as the 1370s. To the right of the bridge was the ford; both of these stood on a wide medieval road which made an impressive approach to the village. Later, as the population increased, the road was made narrower, leaving waste area on both sides which tenants could use, but in the 18th century the Lord of the Manor began to enclose this land and build on it.

50. A peep through the gates of the Clock House at the turn of the century when the property was surrounded by shrubbery and railings. Originally an adjunct of New Place which stood further back, the building provided a time-keeper for the village set in a belfry. It outlived New Place itself, which was demolished in June 1924.

51. Cranham church.

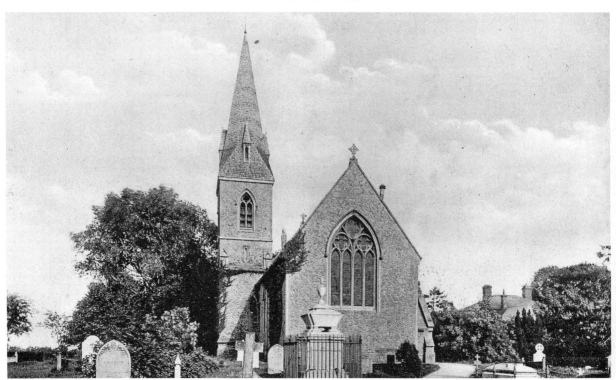

52. Cranham church and the Hall next door will always be associated with General James Oglethorpe (1696-1785), the founder of the state of Georgia in the U.S.A. Having married Elizabeth Wright, heiress of this very old manor, Oglethorpe eventually retired here and spent his last years receiving visitors such as Oliver Goldsmith, Dr. Johnson and Boswell.

Published Sept 9, 1785 by I. Carr, Nº 98 Strand.

53. Cranham Road (now St Mary's Lane) is well wooded in this view. Interest is added by the inclusion, on the right, of Upminster's historian T. L. Wilson – seen resting on his walking stick.

54. The farmhouse known as Great Sunnings is one of the oldest in Upminster. Situated on the east of Sunnings Lane, Corbets Tey, it was marked on the Chapman and André map of 1777 but in the wrong position. In 1896 four rooms were decorated with such panelling, probably from the Jacobean period.

The Ordinary Lot

M. Newman Harding's Pedal for not breaking the Straw

55. What the well-dressed farm labourer in Hornchurch was wearing in 1806. He is operating Mr. Newman Harding's thrashing mill, worked by a foot pedal designed to function without breaking the straw. The mill had been constructed by two young millwrights from Somerset who were paid 50 guineas for the work, including the provision of the iron for the job; Mr. Newman Harding provided the timber.

56. a) (*previous page*) Damyns Hall Farm, *c.*1926, and, in front, the old rose garden. This ancient house was burnt down in 1956.
b) (*above*) George Paveley and a stallion called Boxer in front of the stables behind Damyns Hall Farm. He had been horseman to Mr. Vellacott, the farm owner, but later leased it and took over day-to-day management.
c) (*left*) Edward Paveley, George's son, who was born on the farm and took over management in 1936.

57. The road from Hornchurch village has descended Grey Towers Hill to cross the bridge near the Ravensbourne leading to Harrow Hill. The trees and the telegraph poles in this photograph, *c*.1914, symbolise the balance between rural past and technological future.

58. For centuries weary farmworkers made their way home along this lane. Still overhung with trees in this early 20th-century view, it quickly filled up with houses for clerks and City workers.

59. A sylvan view of North Street, north of Westland Avenue, *c*.1908. Most of the children are in their Sunday best and probably on their way home from Sunday School.

60. Cramped and far from ideal conditions prevailed in these houses on the right at the High Street end of North Street. Somehow large families were raised with several children sleeping in one small room. Despite such limited accommodation, the children often seemed cheerful and alert, as in photographs like this.

61. High Street, 1908. The interesting houses on the left, past the Billet Lane corner, were originally part of Pennants Almshouses, a mellow brick building put up in 1720 which was the Hornchurch Workhouse for many years. The charity was founded in 1590 by Pierce Pennant, Gentleman Usher to Elizabeth I, whose memorial with its quaint inscription can be seen in the church.

62. Further along the High Street is the *Bull Inn*, believed to date from the 16th century. The weatherboarded cottage at the far left was also an ancient structure, demolished in 1950. The famous Hornchurch cricket team dined at the *Bull* at the height of their fame: 'The gentlemen then retired to the *Bull Inn*, where after partaking of a most excellent dinner provided by [George] Gooch the landlord, they were amused by some excellent songs, and the evening passed off with the greatest conviviality'.

63. Shops on the south side of the High Street with a view back to North Street corner. At the far left is Beards the bakers and, beyond, the shop of T. Pearce which contained a forge and a general and furnishing ironmongery.

64. Behind the *White Hart Inn* and its neighbouring houses was the original exit from Station Lane for vehicles and, in this case, a route march. The Church Lads' smart turn out in 1908 anticipates that of soldiers-in-earnest a few years later in the same location (see plate 130).

65. Opposite the old entrance to Station Lane, seen in
plate 64, this group of buildings stood right on the
roadway. Their site is now occupied by a wider pavement.
The cottage on the right was known as Punch's Castle, an
18th-century dwelling, home of a Waterloo veteran called
Mason who sold pails of spring water from the Dell round
the village for ½d. a time.

66. As recently as the First World War Blind Lane, at the
bottom of Station Lane, was still completely rural. It
provided a way through the hedges where Suttons
Gardens are today.

67. Workers and lorry at the sand pit in Suttons Lane, *c.*1920. Note the primitive, almost Heath Robinson-type loading contraption.

68.   A picturesque spot that had resisted centuries of change, seen here in 1910. The Hornchurch Post Mill was burned down on the night of 25 June 1921. A predecessor stood on this site as early as 1294. The Mill Cottage still stands, a fortuitous survivor from the 16th century.

69.   A group of men outside Dury Falls on the Hornchurch Road just before 1914. A succession of horse-drawn vehicles toils up the hill. Are they members of a men's club, awaiting the arrival of a wagonette for a day out (note the umbrella) or are they attending a meeting at the house with Thomas Gardner, J.P.?

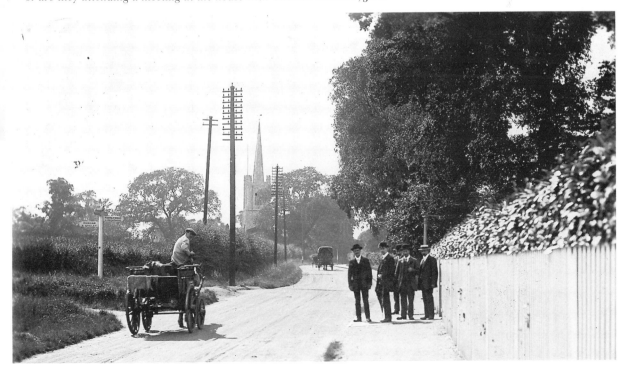

70. Another view of Doggett's Corner showing the 16th-century Dury Falls and the entrance to Wingletye Lane. The photographer must have put a ladder against the direction post, seen in the previous picture, to get a high view. The name of the house derives from the 14th-century Doryval family.

71. The dusty road beckons the weary traveller up Wingletye Lane. Pilgrims to Canterbury may have used this road, passing hamlets such as Hay Green.

72. The carter with a load of hay passes isolated houses at Upminster Bridge, *c*.1910.

73. A procession including firemen and scouts winds its way out of Station Road, Upminster, in the 1920s. On the left a varied collection of carts fills Aggiss's yard, around the Chestnuts. On the right, next to Cosy Corner, a school warning sign indicates increased traffic.

74. The British School was designed to accommodate 150 children, whilst the National School opposite was built for 100 pupils. Both these schools were opened in 1851. The sites in Station Road have now been redeveloped.

75. A quiet day in Station Road, Upminster, 1906. It is hard to believe that the arrival of the railway has had any impact on the village. The station bridge rises in the distance, leading to rural Hall Lane.

76.   A workman smiles at the camera from the tree-lined solitude of Hall Lane. The monks of Waltham Abbey knew this lane in medieval times when Upminster Hall acted as a sanatorium for sick monks.

77.   The mill on Upminster Common in the 19th century.

78. Charlie Baker's shop on Upminster Hill was a Grocery, Drapery and Provision Stores – quite a sophisticated shop for its time. This area started to be developed in the Edwardian period, creating a demand for improved shopping facilities.

King Willow and Other Diversions

79.   Daniel Mendoza, the first Jewish 'Champion of the World', came to the Dell, Hornchurch, to defend his heavyweight title in 1795. The Dell was a natural arena, accommodating 3,000 spectators, and a 24-ft. stage was set up in the middle. The fight was won by Mendoza's opponent Gentleman John Jackson in nine rounds. Mendoza had been the 16th heavyweight champion of the old prize ring and had defeated about 32 opponents before this fight.

EXPLANATORY DIAGRAM OF THE GAME OF CRICKET.

The Batsmen, or Striker.   2. The Bowler.   **3.** The Wicket-keeper.   4. Point (of bat).   5. Short Slip.   6. Long Stop.   7. Long Slip.   8. Middle Wicket.   9. Long Field straight off.   10. Long Field straight on.   11. Long Field cover to point and Middle Wicket 12. Long Field to the Hip.   13. 13. Umpires.   14 Scorers.   X X Bowling Crease.   † † Popping Crease.

THE CHAMPION CRICKET CLUB. — The Hornchurch players have attained the appellation of conquerors in the game, from the extraordinary circumstance that they have been victorious in every match for the last *eight* seasons. This almost unparalleled success has, it appears, induced the country gentlemen to avoid coming in contact with this club, and it would seem, from the few challenges they have of late received, that the palm of victory is to remain with them. Emboldened by this continued success, undisputed by any single club, the Hornchurch club now have the courage to offer to play any picked *eleven in this county.* Will not this offer be accepted? What, we would ask, has become of the Pattiswick and Maldon clubs; whose character and success at one period so far exceeded every other in the county? The season is not too far spent to admit of a match being played, and we shall be surprised indeed, if we are not authorised next week to announce that the challenge has been met. In the mean time we give the particulars of the return match played at Chelsea, between that club and the Hornchurch, the result of which most certainly will give to any but first rate players but little hopes of arresting so victorious a career.

CHELSEA.

	First Innings.		Second Innings.
Seymour	5 run out		15 b. Stevens, sen.
Grieg	1 b. Dow		2 b. Dow
H. Newman	9 b. ditto		3 c. Stevens, jun.
J. Newman	1 c. Adlam		7 leg before wicket
Pitts	15 c. Thompson, jun.		4 st. Terry
Perry	2 b. Dow		0 not out
Howard	3 run out		0 c. Stevens, sen.
Flemming	0 run out		11 b. Adlam
Burt	0 st. Terry		6 c. Thompson, jun
T. Cristmass	0 run out		1 c. Stevens, sen.
Ward	0 not out		0 b. ditto
	36		**49**

HORNCHURCH.

	First Innings.	Second Innings.
Thompson, jun.	25 c. Howard	
Terry	0 b. Seymour	5 not out
Adlam	0 b. ditto	3 b. Flemming
Dow	6 b. H. Newman	
Thompson, sen.	9 b. Seymour	
J. Bearblock	13 run out	
Stevens, jun.	9 not out	4 not out
Stevens, sen.	0 leg before wicket	
G. Bearblock	0 b. Flemming	
West	7 b. H. Newman	
P. Bearblock	2 c. Pitts	
Byes	3	
	74	**12**

Hornchurch winning with 9 wickets to go down.

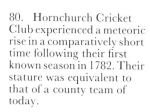

80. Hornchurch Cricket Club experienced a meteoric rise in a comparatively short time following their first known season in 1782. Their stature was equivalent to that of a county team of today.

81. Some men spent what leisure time they had in the public house. The *King's Head* was in a particularly convenient position, just across the road from Hornchurch Brewery. A line up of staff traditionally included the best customer – perhaps the very tall, well-built man on the right.

82. Billiards was the appeal of the *White Hart*. This attractive Victorian building replaced a rambling 15th- or 16th-century inn which was destroyed by fire on the night of 7 November 1872.

83. The *Spencers Arms* at Ardleigh Green was patronised by the local farm workers when this early 20th-century photograph was taken. Here it looks rather bleak, but no doubt the interior was warm and welcoming.

84. Union flags are much in evidence among the children taking part in this celebration at the junction of High Street and North Street.

85. Mrs. Gardner fires the first shot at the opening of the new rifle range while a marshal makes sure there are no accidents, 27 May 1912. The range was situated in Suttons.

86. Preparations for the carnival about 1911, with a haystack in the background. Albert Parrish was a carman or carrier with premises in Station Lane, Hornchurch.

87. Waiting for the carnival procession. This expectant group is standing by the old weatherboarded houses in the High Street, near the North Street corner. A. Smith, the newsagent, published a number of postcard views of the village, and Franklin's the Cobblers were an old established firm in the High Street.

88. The end of the carnival procession, coming down Church Hill. This photograph gives a good view of old Hornchurch Brewery with its massive walls and gates, together with a glimpse of the house inside. Nelmes Farm Dairy (Banyards) cart is nearest the camera, followed by a comic fire brigade tableau.

89.   Hornchurch Football Club in 1906. This photograph was taken in the field opposite Charles Frost, the carriage builders' premises. The club acquired the nickname 'The Urchins'.

90.   An Upminster football eleven, 1920/1. This interesting photograph includes no less than seven officials or supporters plus the small boy in a very natty coat.

91. A 1920s cricket eleven from Upminster which has at least one member in common with the football team. Note the chirpy scorer, pencil fixed behind his ear. Upminster cricket club was formed in 1858 and revived in 1883.

92. Many walks could be taken through the attractive countryside around Hornchurch and Upminster. Visible from more than one footpath were these bridges over the Ravensbourne stream, meandering through the Grey Towers estate.

93. Station Road. Alfred Rendle, a nurseryman from Nags Head Lane, set up these premises selling garden plants in about 1921. In 1927 Mr. Pudney took over. It is remarkable that he was allowed to leave so little pavement for the pedestrians. Gardening was already a leisure pursuit, shopping just becoming one. Looking across the way we see Roomes Stores confined to one building – expansion would not be long in coming.

94.   What a lot of effort has gone into the presentation of these young ladies of the Young Helpers League, seen here at The Court, Upminster, in about 1910.

Stirrings

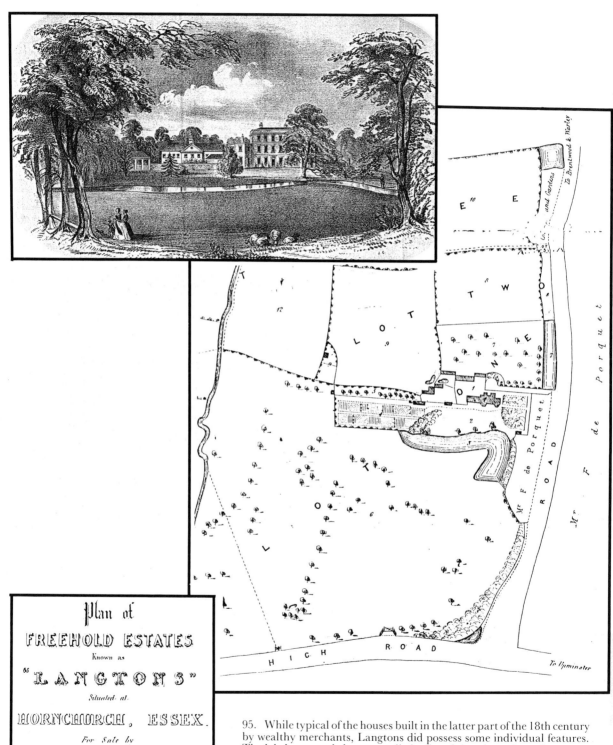

Plan of
FREEHOLD ESTATES
Known as
"LANGTONS"
Situated at
HORNCHURCH, ESSEX.
For Sale by
MESSRS HUMPHREYS AND WALLEN.
1850.

95. While typical of the houses built in the latter part of the 18th century by wealthy merchants, Langtons did possess some individual features. The lake's unusual shape was distinctive, fed perhaps from the same source as the workhouse pond at the bottom end of nearby Billet Lane. The house was owned by the Massu family, Huguenot silk traders in the City of London.

96.   Mary Wedlake continued the business founded in 1784 by her deceased husband and his brother. As manufacturers of agricultural implements, the firm became famous countrywide; indeed several implements were invented and patented by Thomas Wedlake.

THE BARKING AND PITSEA EXTENSION RAILWAY : VIEWS ON THE LINE.

97. 'On Thursday the 11th inst. [11 October 1883], at the pleasant Essex village of Upminster ... the first turf was cut of a new line of railway direct from Barking to Pitsea, by which the journey between London and Southend will be greatly shortened, while this passenger line will be free in comparison with the existing line running further south through Purfleet, Grays and Tilbury, from the inconvenience that might else be occasioned by the merchandise traffic of the new docks, now under construction on the banks of the Lower Thames'.

98. When the Barking-Upminster section of railway line was opened on 1 May 1885 there was no special celebration. Here is Hornchurch station, 20 years later, from the south, tucked away in a country lane.

99. Hornchurch station from the north, soon after the turn of the century. Ind Coope's Ales are on sale from a refreshment room. The *Station Hotel* was not built until 1934. Near the station were the football field and a rifle range, whose targets were concealed inside a high bank.

100. Stationmaster and signalbox staff pose proudly at the end of Hornchurch platform.

101. How the Great Eastern Railway tried to steal traffic from the London, Tilbury and Southend line. The signboard tells the story. Emerson Park Halt on the L.T.S.R. had been opened in October 1909. Gidea Park, at first called Squirrels Heath and Gidea Park, followed on 1 December 1910.

102. The exterior of the old Upminster station, with its first entrance in the station yard. There is none of the bustle usually associated with railway stations and you can almost smell the wild flowers on the waste ground in front of the two onlookers.

103. An early view of Upminster station from the footbridge across the line, with a train about to depart from Barking.

CURIOUS NESTING PLACE,
COACH L.T.&S.R. No 242
UPMINSTER APRIL 9TH 1906.
PHOTO H. AGGISS

104. A conflict between progress and nature in 1906. A bird has nested in the undercarriage of a railway coach which normally shuttles between Upminster and Tilbury. Henry Aggiss was on hand to record the incident.

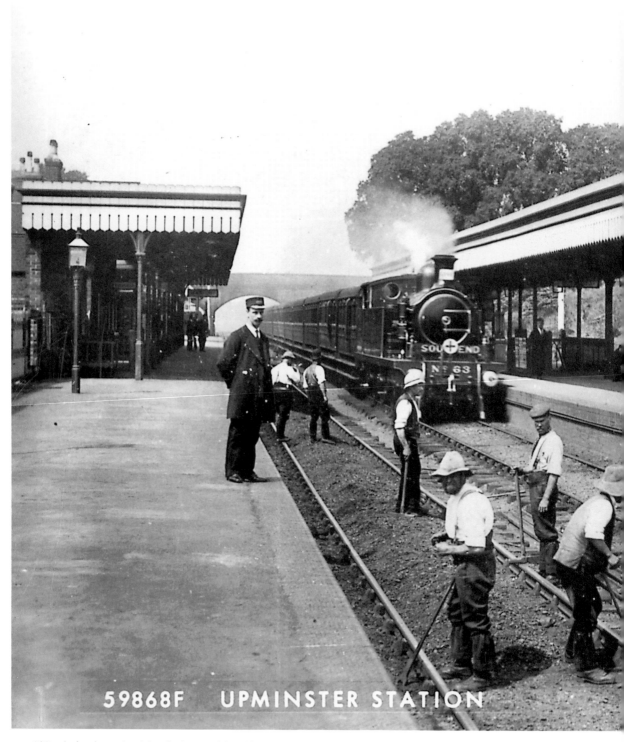

59868F UPMINSTER STATION

105. A classic study of the platforms with uniformed staff, passengers, and platelayers awaiting the approaching train. Notice the beautiful turn-out of the locomotives on the L.T.S.R. at this time.

106. A view of Church Street Hill (now part of High Street). In the centre part of the great mass of brewery property can be seen. In the foreground, shops have been built into the houses on either side of the road. On the right is Rumsey's shop, advertising tyres, a vulcanising service and a public telephone. This gave the name to Rumsey's Corner at the entrance to Station Lane, just out of sight.

107. Roneo Ltd. had established itself, at the beginning of the century, at the far western end of the parish, on a site originally used by a bicycle factory. Here, workers pose with the Foden steam lorry and trailer.

108.   Hill House School, Upminster Hill. This impressive building started in 1792 as a girls school, and in the middle of the 19th century was believed to be one of the finest in Essex. It is now demolished.

109.   Park Lane School, only a few years old when these pupils were captured for posterity by a photographer. The building had been erected in 1893 for £4,000.

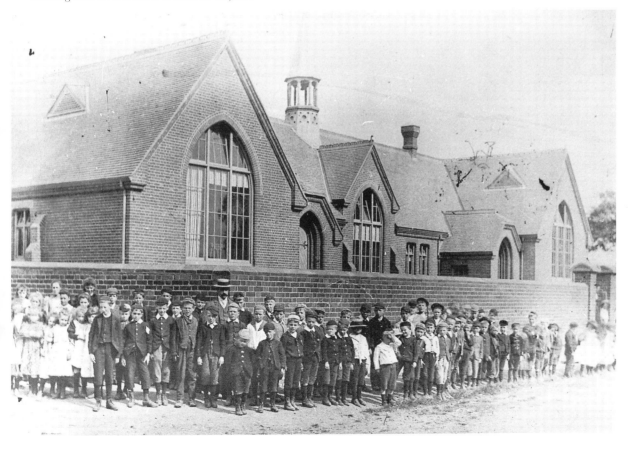

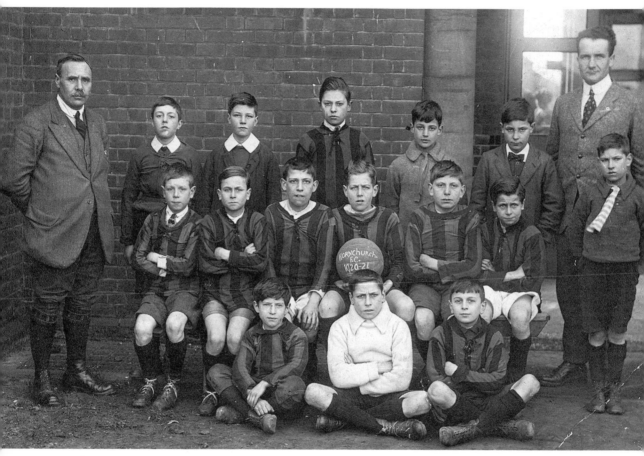

110. The football team representing the Hornchurch village school (now called Langtons) in 1920/21. Back row, left to right: Mr. Frank Edwards, Head Master, known disrespectfully as 'fatty', Bert Cook, Ken Coppin, J. Abrahams, Jack Bruce, Brooks and Frank Doe with Mr. Davies behind. Middle row: Fred Bruce, Frank McLaurin, George Creasy, Will Bruce (Capt.) Brewer, Alec McLaurin. Front row: Johnny Archer, Arthur Hare, Fred Wright.

111.   A group of children at the St Leonard Cottage Homes: why was the little boy standing on his own? The children frame a view of many of the cottages run as 'family' units, and also the sculpture group on the pediment which was brought from Shoreditch. The St Leonard's Homes were built in 1889 to provide a model village environment where children being looked after by the parish could grow up away from the harmful influences of the city. The children were trained to gain employment when they left the homes. There was instruction in bakery, gardening, shoemaking, painting, tailoring and carpentry for the boys, and in cookery, laundry and needlework for the girls.

112.   Shoreditch decided that children in local authority care should be housed away from the inner-city workhouse environment. This photograph shows Edward James Wakeling, Chairman of the Shoreditch Cottage Homes Committee, laying the foundation stone of the new Band Room, Drill Hall and Infants' School Room at Hornchurch on 3 November 1911. Band training was considered a useful recreation and discipline for children and, although the Homes have been closed, there are still many marching bands in the Havering district today.

113.   In 1895 William Carter of Parkstone, Dorset, bought 200 acres of Nelmes manor and neighbouring land and began to develop the Emerson Park estate. By about 1905 his company, Homesteads Ltd., had constructed more than 200 houses in Parkstone Avenue, Herbert Road and Ernest Road. The creation of the Nelmes Estate Garden Suburb was, like all such schemes, an attempt to improve on previous communities and its success is still evident in parts of the estate today. This is a view from Berther Road to the distinctive shops by the station.

114.   This house in Woodland Avenue was originally occupied by a Mr. Brown who was a noted bulb grower. He called it 'Bloemendaal'.

115. Half an Hour from the City: Edwardian advertisements encourage the purchase of land and houses 'in a beautiful rural suburb'.

Half an Hour From the City.

Those who appreciate the charm of living in a beautiful rural Suburb within easy reach of the City will be delighted with UPMINSTER. Situated on a slight eminence in the most picturesque and healthy part of Essex—possessing all the essential features of an ideal residential neighbourhood, and having an excellent increased train service to Fenchurch-street, Moorgate-street and St. Pancras, which runs up to Town in half an hour—UPMINSTER offers exceptional opportunities to business men and health seekers.

UPMINSTER

is quickly developing into a beautiful Town where Real Estate is rapidly rising in value. A few excellent large Freehold Plots may still be purchased for Ten Guineas.

There is no compulsion to build—no tithe or land tax—no restrictions—no law costs —no extras. To those who are unable to obtain the benefits of Life Assurance the exceptional value of these Plots offers an unique, safe and progressive investment for one moderate initial outlay or a few convenient instalments.

The majority of the Estate is already sold, and the remainder will be sold by auction on Saturday afternoon, June 20th, at 4.30 o'clock p.m. in a Marquee on the Estate. A Resident Agent is always available. A few rail tickets are issued to desirable applicants who wish to personally inspect the property, upon personal application. Write or call at once for fullest particulars, plans and special rail tickets to

The Land Co., 68, Cheapside, London, E.C.

116. A view of the windmill and the beginning of development in Cranbourne Gardens, 1907, taken from the church tower by Henry Aggiss.

117. More development in progress, 1906. The road line is being marked out and new houses will soon be started.

118. New fences and a mortgage: Deyncourt Gardens in 1907. The road surface leaves much to be desired.

119. Engayne Gardens: an Edwardian idyll.

120. Delivery of alcoholic drinks from the *Bell Inn* by hand cart, *c.*1910. The houses are very new at this time.

121. Looking past St Lawrence Road to the Market Shopping Centre in Station Road. The children have stopped for the photographer, but an adult has moved too quickly.

A World Swept Away

122. The Sportsmen's Battalion marching down Harrow Hill to their new camp at Grey Towers, 4 November 1914, capes slung across their bodies. The battalion had come by train from Liverpool Street. Hornchurch became, for the first time in its history, the site of a wartime camp.

123. Arriving at the gates by the lodge, the battalion marched in splendid order up the Avenue, led by the boys of the Cottage Homes Band. A large welcoming party from the village was stationed at the entrance. Raised by Mrs. Cunliffe-Owen, the battalion had obtained a special concession for men up to 45 years of age to join. The qualification was usually ability in some kind of sport or entertainment. The battalion included a champion sculler, county cricketers, a scratch golfer, a champion walker, crack-shots, a big-game hunter and boxers, as well as several sporting all-rounders, actors, writers and an archaeologist.

124. The only winter the Sportsmen spent in camp proved to be a snowy one. The Sportsmen made the village seem a busy place: they trained hard, undertaking early morning, pre-breakfast runs through local lanes.

125. Grey Towers Mansion, with Union Jack flying and sentry alert, where battalion officers were quartered. This view shows the carriage porch. Before the war the house had been the home of Colonel Henry Holmes.

The Sportsman's Battalion at Hornchurch.   Sport & General

126.   A group picture of hutmates, taken to satisfy the new interest in army life among the readership of weekly magazines. The soldiers entered into the social life of the district; hardly a week went by without the organisation of a ball, dance or concert, to which the men were invited or in which they participated.

127.   The photographer, Bursall Tonge, was also busy recording the inside story, for posterity and for postcard enthusiasts. There was a growing demand for postcards, partly because they cost less to send than letters. Delivery anywhere in the country could be achieved in a single day and locally it was even possible to get a reply by post within the day.

INTERIOR OF HUT THE CAMP HORNCHURCH.   B. Tonge Hornchurch

Sport & General

"Washing up th

The Sportsman's Battalio

128. Another photocall opportunity: to see men washing up was in itself a novelty.

nner plates".

t Hornchurch.

129.   Local photograher, Frank Luff, who had premises in the High Street, took this view. It shows Colonel Maitland, the Commanding Officer, who in the best battalion traditions unbent at the 1914 Christmas concert by dancing a Highland sword dance and a reel wearing a magnificent Highland costume.

130.   The battalion often marched to and from the station, with their band and pipers at the head of the procession, having spent the day in trench practice at some distant location along the railway line. This photograph was taken at the High Street (or Church Hill) end of Station Lane where Church Lads marched earlier (see plate 64). The chapel in the centre background was only demolished in recent times.

"At the meat store."

131. The beef of old England was certainly on the menu at Grey Towers, but when the boys got to France it would be bully beef out of a tin, if they were lucky. This postcard was sent on 18 February 1915 by a soldier at the camp to a friend.

132. Haynes Park was also used as an army camp. Shown here are the stables adapted from a basic army hut unit.

133. Several views have survived of the funeral procession for Private Alfred Thomas Hills of the South Winnipeg Rifles on 6 May 1915. The Sportsmen's band and a guard of honour accompanied the hearse. Hills had been wounded on 22 April, dying in Oxford Hospital on 2 May. A former choirboy at St Andrew's, he was buried with full military honours in the churchyard. The Sportsmen themselves were soon to depart to France – on 26 June 1915.

134. At the extreme western end of Hornchurch parish, Roneo Ltd. was playing its part in the war effort by supplying munitions. Practically the whole output of the factory was devoted to war purposes. Thousands of duplicators and gallons of ink and similar supplies were made available to the British and Allied cause. Under Government control, the first work comprised the supply of field kitchens; later came dial-sights, automatic machine gun parts, fuses, grenades, shell parts, trench stoves and even aeroplane equipment.

135. The Royal Flying Corps take over Suttons Farm. The temporary RE5 canvas hangars in the background were later replaced by more permanent wooden ones. Tom Crawford, the farmer whose land had been requisitioned, continued to farm an unused part of his farm.

136. Tempest, Leefe Robinson and Sowrey: the three musketeers, who were to bring worldwide fame to Hornchurch.

137. (*above left*) One of the many postcards which appeared after Lieutenant Leefe Robinson destroyed the first German airship (a Schutte Lanz) over Britain on the night of 2/3 September 1916. As Perfect says, 'probably no single incident during the war caused a greater sensation'. The Zeppelins had dominated the sky over Britain for many months and the news of the incident brought renewed confidence to the people of Great Britain.

138. (*above right*) The *London Gazette* for 5 September 1916 announced 'His Majesty the King has been graciously pleased to award the Victoria Cross to ... Lieutenant William Leefe Robinson ... for most conspicuous bravery. He attacked an enemy airship under circumstances of great difficulty and danger and sent it crashing to the ground as a flaming wreck. He had been in the air for more than two hours and had previously attacked another airship during his flight'.

139. (*below*) The machine in which Robinson brought down the SL21 at Cuffley. His two air mechanics stand on either side of part of the wreck. Two hours seems a long time to be in flight in such a flimsy machine and his petrol was almost exhausted on his return from the V.C.-winning trip. Two weeks later he had another lucky escape when this aircraft hit a hedge, burst into flames and was written off.

140. Five flying pals, two ground-crew, an aircraft and wooden hangars. Notice the cavalry-type trousers and boots worn by the officers and the Suttons Farm buildings in the background.

141. Robinson and Sowrey were often to be seen racing through the country lanes of Hornchurch and Upminster in Robinson's Vauxhall 'Prince Henry'. Perfect records the sequel to the destruction of a second Zeppelin: 'presently Capt. Robinson's car came tearing up the lane filled with officers from the Aerodrome, amongst them being the hero of the night, Lieut. Frederick Sowrey. With him were Capt. Robinson, Capt. Stammers, Capt. Bowers and Lieut. C. C. Durston. They were on their way to visit the ruins of the burning Zeppelin lying at Billericay'.

142. When Robinson shot down the first German airship, plans were made to present him with a silver cup. The other two airmen from Suttons bagged their Zeppelins while preparations were going ahead and they were speedily included in the presentation, for whom two more cups had to be purchased. The New Zealand flag reveals that the event was held at Grey Towers. Here Robinson has received his cup from W. H. Legg, Chairman of the parish council (out of the picture), and is being congratulated by Thomas Gardner who is presiding.

143. The presentation over, Robinson (nearest the camera) and Sowrey talk informally with the principal officials. Tempest was on duty and unable to attend the ceremony.

144. After a brief occupation by the Pioneers Battalion, Grey Towers camp became the H.Q. of the New Zealand Soldiers' Convalescent Hospital. The photograph shows the camp in the snowy winter of 1916/17. The back of this postcard contains some lines written in March 1917 by a 'blue boy' wounded in France, to his aunt. He looks forward to being discharged back to New Zealand and comments that his mates are envious of the many parcels he receives, containing cakes and other gifts. He also writes, 'I hold the record for letters too'.

145. The hospital did not lack facilities. A convalescent soldier wrote on the back of the postcard, 'This is the Gymnasium where we get all sorts of exercise for stiff joints. Boat pulling, bicycle riding & other things'.

146.   The Y.M.C.A. hut in the camp. The money came from the New Zealand branch of this organisation, anxious to boost morale among their boys. The Y.M.C.A. block originally consisted of an excellent canteen, billiard room, a large hall seating 800-900, an arts and craft workshop, and a large reading and writing room.

147.   Nine ladies behind the counter of the Y.M.C.A. buffet. The two men with them may be the Camp Secretaries of the Y.M.C.A., Horace Fawcett and P. W. Bushnell. Gradually new facilities were added to the Y.M.C.A. block. By 1918 there were two substantial workshops, seven education rooms and a motor engineering shop for educational purposes.

148.   This canteen was staffed primarily by New Zealand ladies, though assisted 'by ladies of the old country', as Perfect puts it. The colonial troops were of course very popular with local girls at the social events which were held at the camp and in the village.

149. Winter sports were in vogue at Grey Towers during the cold weather of 1916/17; this view shows a mixed crowd of New Zealanders, nurses and some locals including a policeman.

150. 'Te Whare Puni' (The Meeting House) developed from the New Zealanders' Club in London. At first, a small hut in Hornchurch with reading and writing facilities and a buffet was organised by four ladies on 5 March 1916, to provide an oasis of calm for the recuperating New Zealand contingent, where they could obtain a good meal after leaving hospital and relax in a homely atmosphere. Later this house in Butts Green Road was built with the help of army carpenters. It is still standing, having been a private college for a time after the war.

151. A skipping display by Grey Towers nurses, part of a larger entertainment in the parkland. The white costumes give a ghostly, almost surreal, feel to the proceedings.

152. Nurses from the camp are being entertained to tea by Mr. Thomas Gardner of Dury Falls and his wife. Thomas Gardner (who had been elected Chairman of Essex County Council) had taken over the role of 'squire' of the village.

153. The first public demonstration of the new air-to-ground wireless telephony system by 141 Squadron at Suttons Aerodrome in 1918.

154. The Hornchurch Highlanders ready for the Peace Parade at Hornchurch at the end of the First World War.

The March of Progress

155. Aerial view of Upminster, October 1938, showing the many changes which had occurred between the wars. Even so there are plenty of old survivors including the *Bell Inn* and, opposite, Cosy Corner projecting at a much reduced main crossroads.

156. Early 19th-century labourers' cottages behind long front gardens in Corbets Tey Road, *c.*1938. The parade of shops containing Boot's, Woolworth's and latterly MacDonald's was built on the site of these old dwellings.

158. The developers are about to pounce, dividing the land with paling fences in this historic picture of inter-war Upminster (1932/3). Hoppy Hall, believed to date from the 17th century, stands serenely, oblivious of its final fate as a car park, on the far side of Corbets Tey Road.

157. Corbets Tey Road, *c.*1938, with Post Office Cottages (*c.*1780) following the line of the road. Beyond are two modern blocks – the white, gleaming frontage of Springfield Court is the furthest away.

159. The corner of Springfield Gardens and Corbets Tey Road. Hunts, one of the houses built by Sir James Esdaile in 1775, was part of a farm of 130 acres. Seen here in 1933, it was to survive only another four years. A line of shops was built at the roadside.

160. A quiet moment in Upminster Library. The Clock House, St Mary's Lane, was purchased by Upminster parish in 1924 for council offices. After 10 years the parish became part of Hornchurch and the rooms seen here were used as a library until 1963.

161. Upminster had a volunteer fire brigade from 1909, but it was not sufficiently well equipped to tackle large fires so agreements were made for the Hornchurch brigade to assist when the situation demanded. Disagreements over costs caused problems, so when an opportunity arose they re-formed their own volunteer force, appointing a retired professional, John Bridger, as Captain in 1925. In 1927 a motorised engine replaced the old hand truck. The headquarters were, like the library, at the Clock House.

162.   The Capitol Cinema opened on 10 October 1929 with the double bill, 'Parasites' and 'Adams Apple'. St Mary's Lane had changed from the leafy rural backwater seen in plate 53 into an important thoroughfare.

163.   West Central Hornchurch from the air, August 1938. Streets of houses have invaded several parts of the Grey Towers Estate, including the Avenue. Lyndhurst Drive is the long unbroken line across the middle of the picture. Shops and a cinema have replaced trees and fields in the Grey Towers vicinity. In the distance is the grey glitter of Romford.

164. Prince's Park in the fields of South Hornchurch was an estate built as a result of the 1919 Housing or 'Addison' Act (named after the Minister of Health at the time). The Act gave powers and subsidies for the erection of council houses throughout the country, to provide better living conditions for the majority of the populace. Some 171,000 houses were built under this scheme in the years 1919-23, and the Romford Rural District purchased Prince's Farm as a site for council houses.

165. Jack Cornwell's Memorial Houses, Hornchurch. The opening of these houses formed a lasting memorial to the boy V.C. Cornwell's award was won on board the *Chester* at the Battle of Jutland, where he refused to leave his battle station though wounded. He did not survive the action. He joined the Navy aged 15 and died when only sixteen.

166. Survivors! Many of the historic buildings in this view of Hornchurch High Street at the approach from North Street lingered on into the late 1920s and '30s.

167. Workmen preparing for a new road from Station Lane to the High Street. A new line of shops was to be built and eventually a one-way traffice system was introduced around the *White Hart* (now the Madison Exchange).

168. Station Lane – hedges and fields give way to housing.

169. This line of shops was built at the end of Lyndhurst Road to serve the inhabitants of the new roads being built in the 1920s and '30s.

THIS PROMINENT SITE
SOLD BY
HEALEY & BAKER
HAYWARD & C.

170. The end is nigh. The old Britannia block about to be bulldozed to make way for Montague Burton's, the chain tailors, September 1938.

171. Further demolition of Hornchurch's heritage: High Street, opposite the *Bull*, August 1938.

172. Celluloid nights. Hornchurch's second cinema brings modern film glamour to the neighbourhood with a display of light, 3 August 1935. The grand café upstairs held a great attraction for the locals. This cinema brought the village to the threshold of a new age, where international concerns would play a dominant role and newsreels would follow, week by week, the momentous events in Europe.

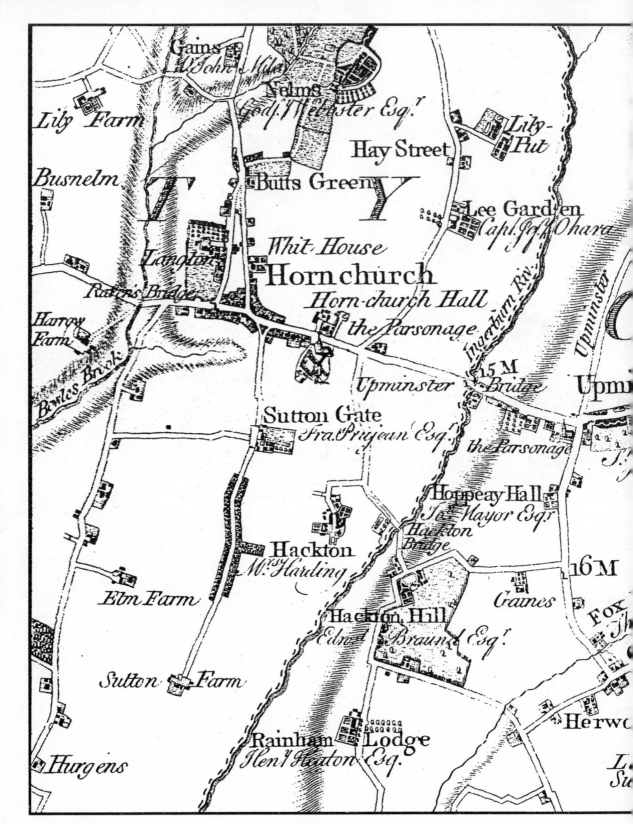

Hornchurch and Upminster on the Chapman and André map, 1777.